This book is dedicated to our beautiful niece, Kate, who was a wonderful example for others by being the nicest girl in school.

For my mom and dad,
who always modeled the importance of
kindness and generosity.

For my husband,
who continually believes in me
and supports my dreams.

Many thanks to John (Bill) Rallo,
for all his time and technical support.

S.R.

Copyright©2019 by Sally Reichert

All rights reserved. No part of this book may be reproduced or transmitted in any form or by any means, electronic or mechanical, including photocopying, recording, or any information storage and retrieval system, without permission in writing from the publisher, except for the inclusion of brief quotations in an acknowledged review.

ISBN: 978-1-7335015-1-4 (hardcover)
ISBN: 978-1-7335015-0-7 (paperback)
ISBN: 978-1-7335015-2-1 (e-book)

Library of Congress Control Number: 2019903182

All characters and events in this book are fictitious. Any similarity to real persons, living or dead, is coincidental and not intended by the author.

A young boy learns about kindness and empathy after missing out on the opportunity to form a new friendship.
    Subjects: 1. Empathy-Fiction 2. Respect-Fiction 3. Bullying-Fiction
            4. Friendship-Fiction 5. Feelings-Fiction

Printed in the United States of America

Published by Tailgator Press

Email: tailgatorpress@gmail.com

For supplemental materials and more information about Tailgator Press or this author visit tailgatorpress.com

The Paper Heart

A Story About How Words Can Hurt
and
How One Kind Action Can Make A Difference

by Sally Reichert

Hands trembling, Martin entered the principal's office.
He was scared.

"Mr. Higgins says you want to see me."

Martin was in third grade at Rayville Elementary School.

Ms. Lopez, the principal, was tall and strict.
She sat at her desk with a stern look and arms folded.

Ms. Lopez shook her head. "I've been told that
you teased Julian."

"Uh, no, I haven't."

Martin's voice cracked. "It wasn't me."

"Someone heard you tease him, Martin," said Ms. Lopez.

Martin couldn't believe someone had tattled on him.
He looked down at his hands.

Ms. Lopez sighed, "I want you to figure out how you can make this up to Julian. I will stop by your classroom later to see what you plan to do."

Martin nodded and pretended to agree with Ms. Lopez.

Martin thought how he treated Julian was no big deal.
He hadn't been mean to Julian.

Martin had no plans of doing what Ms. Lopez wanted.

Besides, he didn't know what to do to make Julian feel better.

Martin thought about the time when his brother, Randy, wouldn't let him play with him and his friends, so Martin made cookies with his mom. He got to lick the beaters.

Another time, Martin's friend, Joey, asked their classmate, Alex, to play at his house, but didn't ask Martin. Martin's big sister, Nancy, took him for ice cream.

I can't do anything like that for Julian, Martin thought.
What can I do in a few hours?

As Mr. Higgins read the story, Martin remembered the time he had teased Julian when Julian had gotten ten wrong on his spelling test.

Martin didn't see what the big deal was. He was only telling the truth.

Mr. Higgins continued to read the story, and each time Sam was bullied, a piece of the heart was torn off.

Martin recalled the day when Julian came to school in a dirty shirt. Martin had told him he smelled.

Now, Martin rubbed his stomach as it began to churn.

He thought about the time Julian didn't have the money for the class field trip, but Julian got to go anyway.

Martin had told the class that Julian got to go for free because he was poor.

Remembering this, Martin slumped in his chair.

When Mr. Higgins finished reading, only a small piece of the heart was left.

Mr. Higgins asked, "What happened to Sam's heart?"

Mr. Higgins explained, "Some good things and some not-so-good things happen to us. The not-so-good things can hurt our hearts. Sam had bad things happen to him that hurt his feelings. Every unkind act, even small ones, can hurt."

Martin thought about Ms. Lopez's request.
What could I possibly do for Julian?

Martin's class lined up for lunch.

Martin stood up to get in line.

He couldn't believe his eyes! On the floor by his table, lay a dozen pieces of torn, red paper.

Martin was amazed! Where did those come from?

He picked up the pieces of paper and stared at them.

Martin realized the class had left.
He set the pieces of paper on his table
and then hurried out of the classroom.

The class returned from lunch. As they continued their lessons, Martin pondered about what he could do for Julian.

At the end of the day, Mr. Higgins told everyone to say goodbye to Julian. They all watched Julian put his school supplies into his ripped book bag. He would not be returning to Rayville School because Julian's parents were migrant workers and moved often. They traveled to different farms to pick crops.

Martin didn't say a word. He didn't even look at Julian.

As he put his last notebook in his backpack,
Julian found on his table a red, paper heart taped together
with the words "I am Sorry" written on it.

Julian picked it up. He glanced in Martin's direction.
Martin grinned.

Ms. Lopez walked over and put her hand on Martin's shoulder.

"I'm proud of you for finding a way to make things better with Julian."

"I didn't realize I had hurt Julian. I'm sorry," said Martin.

For the first time, Julian left Rayville Elementary School with a smile on his face.

Later that week, Mr. Higgins introduced a new student, Andrew.

Remembering the torn heart, Martin made eye contact with Andrew and grinned.

At lunchtime, Martin invited Andrew to sit with him. They found out they both had annoying sisters.

Martin asked Andrew to play basketball at recess. Andrew taught Martin some quick moves.

Martin chose Andrew to be his science partner. Together, they made the best volcano.

Martin and Andrew became good friends.

This made Martin wonder if he and Julian

could have been good friends if only he had been kinder.

At Rayville School, a young boy named Martin
was in third grade.
He was asked by the principal to correct
the mistakes he had made.

Martin heard a story about how
teasing can hurt the heart.
As his teacher read, piece by piece,
the paper heart broke apart.

Martin thought about his teasing
of Julian and began to feel bad.
He realized he hurt Julian's feelings
and now felt sad.

When Martin stood up for lunch
and stepped in the aisle,
he saw red pieces of paper
on the floor in a pile.

The class said goodbye to Julian
as he would soon leave Rayville School for good.
Martin wondered how to make Julian
feel better because he knew he should.

Martin looked on his desk
at the pieces of red paper he had
and suddenly had an idea
so Julian wouldn't feel so bad.

Julian left school that day with the heart
in his hand and a smile on his face.
Martin realized kindness
was a habit he needed to embrace.

Martin met Andrew
and their friendship grew fast.
Being kind was the way
a friendship would last.

Martin thought about Julian
and the lesson he learned:
By being kind,
a friendship can be earned.

- Pam DeGroot
- Sally Reichert

CPSIA information can be obtained
at www.ICGtesting.com
Printed in the USA
BVHW091729171119
563996BV00003B/9/P